Let's work together

A practical guide for schools to involve parents and carers in sex and relationships education

Lucy Emmerson

The Sex Education Forum is the national authority on sex and relationships education (SRE). It is a unique collaboration of over 90 member organisations and 750 practitioners with representatives from health, education, faith, disability and children's organisations. We believe that all children and young people have the right to good SRE and aim to provide all professionals involved in SRE with the information they need to ensure this right.

If you work with young people, in school or in a youth or community setting as a teacher, health professional, social worker or you are a parent or carer we can help provide you with the information and support you need to provide effective sex and relationships education. Visit www.sexeducationforum.org.uk for more information or email sexedforum@ncb.org.uk.

NCB's vision is of a society in which children and young people contribute, are valued, and their rights respected. Our mission is to improve children and young people's experiences and life chances, reducing the impact of inequalities. NCB aims to:

- reduce inequalities of opportunity in childhood
- ensure children and young people can use their voice to improve their lives and the lives of those around them
- improve perceptions of children and young people
- enhance the health, learning, experiences and opportunities of children and young people
- encourage the building of positive and supportive relationships for children and young people with families, carers, friends and communities
- provide leadership through the use of evidence and research to improve policy and practice.

NCB has adopted and works within the UN Convention on the Rights of the Child.

Published by NCB

NCB, 8 Wakley Street, London EC1V 7QE
Tel: 020 7843 6000
Website: www.ncb.org.uk
Registered charity number: 258825

NCB works in partnership with Children in Scotland (www.childreninscotland.org.uk) and Children in Wales (www.childreninwales.org.uk).

First edition

ISBN: 978 1 909391 07 9

British Library Cataloguing in Publication Data

A catalogue record for this book is available from the British Library

Typeset by Saxon Graphics Ltd, Derby
Printed by Cambrian Printers, Aberystwyth

Acknowledgements
Sam Beal, Jane Lees, Anna Martinez, Lisa Handy, Lisa Hallgarten, the members of the National teachers SRE Group; in particular Sharon Langrish, Boo Spurgeon and Michelle Quint, Lynnette Smith, Nav Nahal, Malin Stenstrom, Helen Emerson, Julia Jefferson, Marian Mulroy, Alison Browning, Sue Adams, Chris Powley and David Kesterton.

Contents

Introduction

This resource is designed to help primary and secondary schools involve parents and carers in sex and relationships education (SRE). It includes:

- the evidence showing that parents want to get involved and the benefits for children when they do
- practical ideas for supporting parents with their SRE role, including tried and tested examples
- audit questions to use with parents to review school SRE
- activities to use with parents in workshops and meetings.

What is SRE?

Sex and relationships education (SRE) is learning about the emotional, social and physical aspects of growing up, relationships, sex, human sexuality and sexual health. It should equip children and young people with the information, skills and values to have safe, fulfilling and enjoyable relationships and to take responsibility for their sexual health and well-being.

Why is SRE important?

Sexual development and intimate relationships are fundamental aspects of human life, yet many people find them difficult to talk about. Adult embarrassment can prevent children and young people from getting honest answers to their questions. Many children go through puberty and adolescence without a basic understanding about how their bodies work.

Children absorb ideas, attitudes and beliefs about sex and relationships from their family, friends and community, from adverts, television and the internet – even when no-one at home talks about it.

In the 21st century SRE in schools and at home is more important than ever. It ensures that children and young people have a source of reliable information about growing up and an opportunity to explore the messages they are receiving from the wider world in a safe learning environment.

When should SRE start?

Good quality SRE provides structured learning opportunities with consistent messages that are built on year by year. Starting SRE early in primary school enables children and young people to learn what is safe and unsafe and to get help if they need it. SRE helps children and young people to understand themselves and others and to be prepared for the physical and emotional changes of puberty and adolescence. Young people will be more prepared to take responsibility for and enjoy sexual and emotional relationships free from exploitation.

Why work together?

Who is responsible for SRE?

The Sex Education Forum (SEF) believes that SRE is the joint responsibility of school and home. The majority of parents also see it as a dual responsibility (Durex and others 2010). There are three important reasons for schools to involve parents in SRE:

- to bring about improvements in the SRE children and young people get in school
- to help parents provide better SRE at home
- to support children's and young people's development and well-being by linking learning at school and home.

When schools work together with parents on SRE they often find other benefits too, for example, parents get more involved in children's learning in other subjects.

For information about what schools are legally required to teach in relation to SRE, check the info box at the end of this section.

What is the evidence that SRE works?

National and international research shows that good quality SRE has a protective function as young people who have had good SRE are more likely to be older when they first have sexual intercourse, to have fewer sexual partners and to use contraception (Kirby 2007). All those involved in sex and relationships education want young people to wait until they are ready before they start having sex. For some young people, this may not be until they get married – but it is vital that all young people are helped to develop the emotional skills needed to make responsible choices. There is no evidence that teaching children about sex and relationships encourages them to have sex.

The unique role of parents in SRE

Children and young people are clear that parents are an important source of learning about sex and relationships (Turnbull and others 2012). More than three-quarters of parents feel they should have a role as sex and relationships educators – 77 per cent in one study and 90 per cent in another (NHS Bristol 2009 and Ingham and Carrera 1998) but fewer actually talk to their children.

SRE at home can be more informal and spontaneous than timetabled teaching at school. And because of the unique relationship between a parent and child this makes learning about sex and relationships at home very different to school.

The Sex Education Forum spoke to members of a faith and values working group about what makes the role of parents in SRE unique. Their thoughts about the opportunities and challenges involved are shown in the box.

The unique role of parents in SRE
Ideas from members of the Sex Education Forum faith and values working group

Opportunities

- parents have an emotional relationship with their child
- potentially have time to talk
- spontaneous 'here and now' context (e.g. while watching a TV programme)
- parents transmit their personal and community values and views
- developmental approach that can be appropriate to child's age and level of understanding
- unique knowledge of child – although don't know everything
- siblings and other relatives can contribute
- parents can set the tone about sex and relationships before children go to school
- parents can be advocates for good SRE for their children

Challenges

- generational patterns get repeated
- how to respect a child's privacy
- authority and boundary-setting role may mean children keep things from parents – that's the nature of adolescence and parenting
- home is not always a safe place
- depends how confident and comfortable parents are about talking about sex and relationships

> **Most parents give the 'birds and bees' talk when they feel ready, not when the child is ready which seems really weird and parents get embarrassed and tend to give up!** Young person responding to Sex Education Forum survey, 2008
>
> **If we had SRE when we were younger then a lot of us would have been better equipped to deal with a lot of things in life.** Parent speaking at a discussion group about SRE at a primary school in Birmingham

What role do parents really take?

Many parents and carers find it difficult to talk to their children about sex and relationships. As a result many children grow up without ever having had a conversation with their parents about sex and relationships. Boys are less likely than girls to have talked to their parents, and fathers are less likely than mothers to start a discussion.

So there is a big gap between the ideal role that parents aspire to as educators and what happens in reality. Children and young people are well aware of parents' failings with SRE.

> My own mother was brilliant, but parents whose own sex education was lacking will have trouble knowing how best to teach their children.
> Young person responding to Sex Education Forum survey 2008

> I think young people are hardly getting any messages from their parents as they think it is up to the education service to do this, however the education service seem to think it is up to the parents.
> Young person responding to Sex Education Forum survey 2008

Why do parents fail to fulfil the role they aspire to?

Embarrassment is a big factor; over half of parents say they find it embarrassing to talk about sex with their child (Populus 2008). **Lack of knowledge** can also be a barrier because parents are concerned about exposing ignorance on sexual matters to their children (Walker 2001) or believe their children know things already (NHS Bristol 2009).

Parents have also said that **not having a good experience of sex education oneself** makes it harder, although in some cases parents are determined for the cycle to be broken (Turnbull and others 2011, Kirkman and others 2005 and Walker 2001). Some parents report not having had any SRE at all.

Parents are sometimes concerned that talking about sex and relationships may encourage their children to be curious or experimental. However, there is no evidence that this is the case. In fact, research shows that SRE results in young people being older when they first have sex (Kirby 2007).

Some parents have commented that they find it difficult to communicate about sexual matters to older children if there are younger siblings in the family (Turnbull and other 2012).

What role do parents see for schools in SRE?

Most parents (84 per cent) believe that school and home **should both be involved** in SRE. A small percentage of parents (6 per cent) believe that SRE should be taught only at school and 7 per cent believe it should only be taught at home (Durex and others 2010).

So there is widespread support from parents for school to have a role in SRE. As many as **98 per cent** of parents answering a Mumsnet survey said they were happy for their children to attend school SRE lessons (Mumsnet 2011).

Parents have described school SRE as an effective **supplement** to SRE at home (Sherbert Research 2009), in some cases because they have found it difficult to provide it themselves (NFER 1994). A minority of parents express concerns that values taught at school may not be the same as theirs (Sherbert Research 2009).

Parents do not always know what schools are teaching in SRE. Some parental concerns about SRE stem from misunderstandings about the title 'SRE' and specifically what is meant by 'sex' and what is included in teaching. The use of the word 'sex' is sometimes interpreted as relating only to sexual intercourse – not to the wider social and emotional context or even to the broader biological definition. In one survey over a quarter of parents 'didn't know' how well school SRE prepared their child (Durex and others 2010).

The benefits of schools and parents working together on SRE

Research has found that children and young people benefit more from SRE if home and school are both involved (Kirby 2007).

Schools can address parental misunderstanding about what SRE actually is and this can result in more parents being supportive of school provision. Schools can go a step further and work with parents to help them in their SRE role at home. By starting a dialogue with parents, schools can begin to address the factors that limit parental input, such as embarrassment and lack of knowledge.

Partnerships between school and home have been found to help pupils to achieve more in other subjects and the same is true for SRE (see info box 'What the research says'). If parents understand what exactly is being taught in school it enables relevant follow-up at home. This is true of all subjects, but is particularly important with SRE because of the additional barriers to communication such as embarrassment. Also discussion at home about SRE has a particular function because of the personal nature of the subject.

If children and young people know that parents know what they have been taught, it makes it easier for them to ask questions at home about what they have learnt at school. So a strong school–parent partnership also reaps benefits for pupil well-being.

The benefits of schools working closely with parents are recognised in the Ofsted Inspection Framework for Schools (Ofsted 2012). Inspectors look at how well school leaders and managers 'engage with parents and carers in supporting pupils' achievement, behaviour and safety and their spiritual, moral, social and cultural development' (Ofsted 2012). Ofsted has also commented on the general lack of home-school dialogue on SRE (Ofsted 2010).

Parents and carers have unique knowledge of their children and the local community and can therefore help schools to design an SRE programme that truly meets their children's needs.

The combination of SRE at school and home is more than the sum of the parts. At school children and young people will hear the views and opinions of their peers and be taught in the context of clear values of love, care and respect. At home the family's specific values, beliefs, culture and ethos can be communicated through discussions about sex and relationships. Even if there are differences in what is taught at home and school children and young people can start to develop their own understanding and their own views based on what has been said, rather than on what has been left unsaid.

> Parents and carers are often surprisingly open with their children about SRE, but will only talk if prompted – which can be daunting – because they are under the illusion schools cover sex and relationships.
> Young person responding to Sex Education Forum survey 2008

Figure 1: Parents and schools working together on SRE

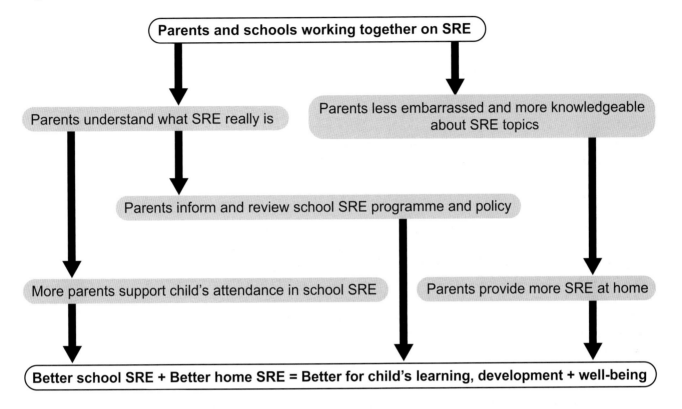

Better school SRE + Better home SRE = Better for child's learning, development + well-being

Info box: What the research says about parental involvement in education

Researchers have found that parental involvement has a positive effect on children's attainment and have examined what kind of involvement makes the most difference and at what age. Desforges found that families have much more impact than schools on attainment when children are at primary age, but this shifts in secondary school and by Key Stage 4 the impact of parental involvement is less than the impact of school (Desforges and Abouchaar 2003). It is therefore essential to intervene at primary age to support parents to get involved in their children's education.

The type of involvement that has most impact on attainment is conversations between parents and children at home. Researchers looked at other types of involvement such as enhancing their child's self-esteem, modelling social and educational aspirations and values, and monitoring out of school activities such as homework. But the conversations parents have with their children at home had more impact than the other types of involvement examined.

Info box: The law relating to SRE in schools

What do schools have to teach?
It is compulsory for all maintained schools to teach some parts of **sex education**, i.e. the biological aspects of puberty, reproduction and the spread of viruses*. These topics are statutory parts of National Curriculum Science, which must be taught to all pupils of primary and secondary age. Parents cannot withdraw their children from this teaching. There is also a separate requirement for secondary schools to teach about HIV and other sexually transmitted infections.

The broader topic of **sex and relationships education** is currently not compulsory but is contained within non-statutory PSHE education. However, when any school provides sex education, teachers and schools must have regard to government SRE guidance (DfEE 2000). School governors must give 'due regard' to this guidance and academies choosing to teach SRE must also have regard to this guidance. Parents have the right to withdraw children from all or part of the SRE taught outside National Curriculum Science.

Schools are legally required to provide a broad and balanced curriculum. The Equality Act 2010 covers the way the curriculum is delivered, as schools and other education providers must ensure that issues are taught in a way that does not subject pupils to discrimination. Schools have a legal duty to ensure the well-being of their pupils and SRE contributes to this duty (Education and Inspections Act 2006 Section 38).

SRE policy requirements
Maintained primary and secondary schools are legally obliged to have an up-to-date SRE policy that describes the content and organisation of SRE taught outside the Science Curriculum. In primary schools if the decision is taken not to teach SRE outside the Science Curriculum this should also be documented in the policy. It is the responsibility of the school's governing body to ensure that the policy is developed and made available to parents.

---

* The most up-to-date legislation relating to SRE is contained within the Education Act (1996) and the Learning and Skills Act (2000).

My daughter has come home and told me that she was called a virgin and she asked me what it meant and was very upset about it. If we have a programme that gives them the right information and parents also know what is being taught then we can all say the same thing and it would eliminate a lot of the teasing and hearsay.

Parent speaking at a discussion group about SRE at a primary school in Birmingham

Summary of key points about parents and SRE

- Children and young people see parents and carers as an important source of information about sex and relationships.
- Most parents feel they should discuss sex and relationships with their children.
- Many parents fail to discuss sex and relationships with their children as much as they wish to.
- Many parents underestimate how much their children want to communicate with them about sex and relationships.
- Fathers are less likely than mothers to talk to their children about sex and relationships.
- The majority of parents support school SRE.
- Some parents are unaware of what SRE is provided at school.
- A small minority of parents choose to withdraw their children from school SRE.
- There is strong evidence that young people who have good quality SRE that starts early are more likely to be older when they first have sex, to have fewer sexual partners and to use contraception.
- Embarrassment, lack of knowledge and poor experience of own sex education are factors that limit parents' communication with their children.
- Some parents are skilful in discussing sex and relationships education.
- The majority of parents want support with SRE and more involvement with school SRE.
- Many schools are failing to involve parents in SRE – but there are examples of good practice.

How to work together: building a dialogue between home and school

Just as parents should avoid having one 'big talk' about sex and relationships with their children, so communication about SRE between parents and schools should be an ongoing conversation and not a one-off. But each school will be at a different point in their SRE journey and some will have communicated about SRE to parents much more than others. So information in this section is divided as follows:

A. How schools can introduce SRE to parents

B. How to maintain ongoing communication between schools and parents

C. How to offer additional support to parents.

Schools will want to pick and mix the approaches that work best for them. For key information about parents' rights in relation to SRE, check the info box on page 13.

A. How schools can introduce SRE to parents

Getting started is often the hardest part, particularly if there has been very little dialogue between school and parents about SRE. A review of the school SRE policy provides a good opportunity to initiate contact with parents. Similarly an event such as the HPV vaccination programme or an e-safety project can be a hook. A quick survey will help gauge parents' responses and assess need. In some cases parents are the ones to set the ball rolling by requesting more information about SRE from the school. Some ideas for getting started are set out below.

Benchmark survey
Carrying out a quick survey with parents can help introduce further discussions about SRE provision at the school and generates useful data against which changes can be measured. Some suggested questions are below.

- Did you know there is a school policy on sex and relationships education (SRE)?

  Yes   /   No   /   Not sure

- Has your child ever talked to you about something they learnt at school to do with growing up, sex and relationships?

  Yes   /   No   /   Not sure

- Has your child ever asked you questions about growing up, sex and relationships?

  Yes   /   No   /   Not sure

- Would you like more information about what the school teaches on sex and relationships?

  Yes   /   No   /   Maybe

- Do you want more support to help you talk to your child about sex and relationships issues at home?

  Yes   /   No   /   Not sure

The survey could be carried out using paper-based questionnaires, online surveys or text message response. For more in-depth research with parents, consider holding focus groups.

Involving parents in a review of the SRE policy

Both primary and secondary schools are legally obliged to have an up-to-date SRE policy that describes the content and organisation of SRE taught outside the Science Curriculum. This applies to all maintained schools in England. Academies are required to have regard to the government guidance on SRE (DfEE 2000) but do not have to have a policy, although they may still choose to do so.

School governing bodies are responsible for the SRE policy and should involve parents and carers in developing and reviewing the policy. A combination of the following methods can be used to involve parents in reviewing the SRE policy.

1 Send the draft policy out to all parents by email, letter or posted on the school website and invite feedback and comments. Asking specific questions will make it easier for parents to respond.

2 Invite parents to a meeting about the policy. This will provide more time to explore what SRE really is and for facilitated activities that help parents to reflect on what kind of SRE they want for their children.

3 Recruit a group of parents (e.g. an existing group of parent helpers) to be a 'task force' and carry out a consultation on the policy. For example, a table could be set up in the playground at 'home time' or during a parents' evening so that the task force can ask other parents one to one about their views on the school policy.

4 Involve pupils in asking their parents for their views on the policy and feed these back through the school council.

The case study below shows how gathering pupil views and then sharing them with parents provided the focus and starting point for a review of a primary school's SRE policy.

Case study: Consulting parents about the SRE policy
The first step in updating the SRE policy at Holy Family Primary School in Birmingham was to inform parents and invite their input. The school also wanted to get the views of children across all year groups. Parents gave permission for their children to be involved in the focus groups. Children were asked about their knowledge on topics such as growing up and where they got their information. The school then arranged a parents' discussion group and shared what the children had said and explained the legal responsibilities that schools and parents have for SRE. The views of parents and children were shared with staff and a new policy was then written with support from the Birmingham Health Education Service. This will be shared with governors for their approval.

Telling parents what children say
Sharing material created by pupils in SRE lessons with parents is a great way to capture attention and gain support. This could take the form of questions asked by pupils that have been posted in an anonymous question box as part of a needs assessment. This will show parents the kind of questions that children of a particular age want to ask.

The Sex Education Forum has produced toolkits for involving primary age and secondary age pupils in reviewing SRE. Materials generated from the activities in these toolkits can be shared with parents. Consider sharing highlights from pupil feedback in a letter home and inviting parents into school for a workshop or ask parents to reply with suggestions about how school and home can work together to meet the needs identified by the children.

Raising awareness about SRE
Before undertaking a full review of the school SRE policy, schools may want to gradually raise parents' awareness of SRE.

This could be achieved by including snippets of information in regular communications produced by the school. For example:

- make a science display of pupils' work on life cycles
- tell parents what the school is doing to mark World AIDS Day
- include a statistic about teenage pregnancy rates in the local area
- share a useful web link or highlight a book that parents can use to discuss sex and relationships at home
- tell parents how the theme from 'anti-bullying week' will be followed up with learning about relationships.

The case study below describes how a small group of parents initiated an SRE awareness raising event for all parents at a secondary school.

Case study: Parents/carers meetings to raise awareness of the sex and relationships education curriculum
Initially, the Parent Link group at Varndean Secondary School in Brighton & Hove requested more information about the school's sex and relationship education programme. This parents/carers group invited all parents to the meeting, but focused on Year 7 parents/carers. The event was also advertised in the school newsletter. The evening was planned by the PSHE coordinator, the local authority Healthy Schools consultant and a Parent Link representative. The planning was designed to enable parents/carers to discuss issues amongst themselves. The outline plan for the event, which lasted one hour, 30 minutes, is shown here:

1 Welcome and warm-up (Human Bingo)

2 Ground rules (focusing on not sharing information about individual parents and students outside of the meeting)

3 Why teach SRE at Varndean School?

   Parents/ carers talk in pairs about their experiences of SRE and whether it was what they needed and at the right time, following up by discussion.

Context for SRE nationally and locally. A normative quiz that highlights key issues, but also reminds parents/carers that most young people do not have sex under the age of 16.

4 Values and attitudes

Attitudes continuum to explore parental attitudes, issues and concerns.

5 School policy and brief overview of curriculum

6 Review of activities (carousel of activities from different year groups introduced by students)

7 Talking to our children about sex

'Top Tips' paired discussion and feedback.

Give out leaflets/booklist.

8 Evaluation

The evening was very positively evaluated with parents/carers reporting they would like more support in talking with their children about sex, drugs, alcohol and e-safety. The school has followed this up and will be repeating this meeting.

From this meeting the school began working in partnership with another local school, Dorothy Stringer School, to host a range of 'Talking to your teens' sessions for parents and carers. This has included talking to your teens about drugs and alcohol and another on e-safety. The joint 'Talking to your teens … about sex and relationships' session was attended by 40 parents and carers from both schools and included latest research on issues such as violence in teen relationships. Parents/carers again evaluated this session positively and particularly appreciated talking with other parents and carers and exploring messages they could give their children at home; including messages about delay and consent.

Parents as advocates for improving SRE

Initial dialogue with parents may produce surprising results. For example, parents are sometimes surprised by how late some topics are introduced in school or how little is covered. Schools may find a group of parents are keen to get involved further. These parents can be an invaluable resource, for example:

- as a sub-group to review the SRE provision at a deeper level
- to gather the views of other parents
- to talk to other parents about SRE, providing reassurance or correcting misunderstandings.

Info box: SRE rights and responsibilities of school and parents

What is the school's responsibility to parents?
The government guidance on SRE (DfEE 2000) emphasises the importance of schools working in partnership with parents.

Under current legislation schools should enable parents to exercise their right to withdraw their children (until the age of 19) from any school SRE taught outside National Curriculum Science. This applies to maintained primary and secondary schools and includes pupils attending a sixth form that is part of a school. It does not apply to sixth form colleges and further education colleges.

Parents have a legal right to see the school SRE policy and to be given a copy of it. It is the responsibility of the school's governing body to develop the policy and to make it available to parents.

Parents should also be aware that schools are legally required to provide a broad and balanced curriculum. Sex and relationships topics can arise incidentally in other subjects and it is not possible to withdraw pupils from these relatively limited and often unplanned discussions.

School communications to parents about their rights
Parents often have little knowledge about what SRE schools provide. Some schools have only communicated with parents about SRE to tell them about their right to withdraw their child. Parents need to understand more fully what SRE is all about to make an informed choice.

It can work well to inform parents about their right to withdraw as part of broader communications about SRE or PSHE. It is advisable to give parents the facility to opt out (not to opt in). Remember that only a minority of parents are likely to consider opting out.

In the rare cases that parents opt out of SRE, schools are strongly encouraged to offer further dialogue, either by letter or at a meeting (a sample letter to parents is provided at the end of the publication). Parents need to be informed of their responsibility to provide SRE at home if they choose to withdraw their child. It is good practice for schools to offer to support parents opting out of school SRE, for example with copies of materials used with pupils in school.

Young people's access to health services at school
A parent's choice to withdraw a child from SRE does not affect the child's right to use confidential health services provided at the school or elsewhere. For further information see the Sex Education Forum factsheet: *Confidentiality: promoting young people's sexual health and well-being in secondary schools* (2007).

B. How to maintain ongoing communication between schools and parents

With home-school dialogue on SRE underway, schools can start to plan regular means of communication that follow the child through their schooling.

Think about how the school communicates with parents about other aspects of school life. Much of the communication about SRE can be built into existing school-home communication channels. Here are some ideas:

1 Include a section on SRE in the school prospectus and information packs for new parents.

2 Summarise what pupils will learn in SRE in the coming weeks in termly updates to parents.

3 Give pupils SRE-related homework, some of which requires input from parents.

4 Report on progression in SRE at parents' evenings or meetings.

5 Use newsletters and the school website to tell parents about special events such as SRE projects to mark World AIDS Day and LGBT (Lesbian, Gay, Bisexual, Transgender) history month.

Case study: Using the virtual learning environment
Each department at Haverstock School, Camden has a virtual classroom where a notice board is set up for students and another for parents. The idea is to encourage more parents to collaborate with the school on how to improve their child's attainment and achievement in all subjects. The PSHEE department plans to use the tool to gauge what parents and students think about SRE. For parents the virtual learning environment (VLE) may be used to assess their views and attitudes about SRE in secondary school, to share the scheme of work and teaching materials and to signpost other sources of help and information. It is also hoped that the VLE will support an internal community of parents, carers and students to suggest improvements to the SRE provision.

Timeline

Primary

- Welcome information from the school includes details of SRE policy (including parental withdrawal).
- Send parents vocabulary lists: words that will be introduced to children in SRE this year including proper names for external genitalia.
- Give parents a list of books that look at 'where babies come from' together with an invitation to look at or borrow books from school.
- Practical information about support for girls who start menstruating, what will be covered in SRE and suggestions for what parents can discuss at home.
- Information about safety online.

Secondary

- Welcome information from the school includes details of SRE policy (including parental withdrawal).
- Information about health and information services that young people can access in school and locally for issues such as body image, self-esteem, sexual health, drugs, alcohol, smoking and relationships.
- Send home a leaflet about the HPV vaccination programme and cervical cancer.
- Invite parents to attend an SRE-related event, for example, a theatre in education performance (together with their children).

Further education

- Welcome information from the college includes details of SRE policy.
- Factsheet about incidence of sexual exploitation, STIs, unplanned pregnancy for young people aged 16–19.
- List of services that can be accessed in school/college and also locally.

Year 1 — Who is the oldest person and who is the youngest person in my family?

Year 2 — What was I like when I was a baby? What made me laugh? What did I look like?

Year 3 — Did you have a best friend? What was their name and what was special about them?

Year 4 — What was the best bit about growing up? What was the worst bit?

Year 5 — How old were you (mum/aunty/stepmum/grandpa etc.) when you started your periods?

Year 6 — Did you keep in touch with your friends from primary school? Did you make new friends at secondary school? Did you have any friends who were very different to you? How old were you (dad/uncle/stepdad/grandpa etc.) when your voice broke?

Year 7 — Do you think it is better to be a teenager now or when you were a teenager? Why?

Year 8 — What kind of SRE did you have at your school? What was good or bad about it?

Year 9 — Have people's attitudes to marriage changed since you were younger?

Year 10 — What is the best bit of advice you got about relationships from your parents or other members of your family?

Year 11 — What is the toughest thing about being a parent and what is the best thing?

Year 12 — Have ideas about the role of men and women in relationships changed since you were at school?

Year 13 —

Termly or weekly:

- Remind parents about what topics will be covered in SRE this week/term.
- Suggest topics for follow-up discussion at home.
- Hold a 'subject surgery' for parents to discuss pupils' progress or issues of concern relating to SRE.

Every year:

- Share updates on school SRE policy.
- Ask parents about topics they think are top priority for their children this year.
- Invite discussion of child's progress in SRE at parents' evening.
- Carry out SRE audit questionnaire with parents (see Activities Part 1: multi-media survey activities).
- Tell parents what topics will be covered in SRE this year.
- Build in an SRE homework activity that involves parents.
- Provide a leaflet or web link giving tips on how to talk to your children.

Let's work together

C. How to offer additional support to parents

With parents clearly in the picture about the SRE in school, it is a good time to consider if more can be done to support parents as educators at home. Research shows that this is something parents really want help with. Activities such as surveys, focus groups and consultation with parents are likely to have revealed particular issues, for example, dads and male carers wanting tailored support to get more involved in SRE at home.

Think about who you want to help and who might get involved. Here are some questions to consider.

- Are you trying to support all parents or targeting particular groups?
- Are there existing groups of parents that are comfortable working together, e.g. dads' groups, grandparents' clubs, cultural or religious groupings?
- How can the parent liaison officer or other specialist staff help?
- Are there local organisations and agencies with relevant expertise in SRE and parenting?
- Is there a local authority SRE advisor who can help?
- What is in the local parenting strategy and can you link with it?
- What are other local schools already doing to support parents with SRE?
- Can you involve the local Sure Start/Children's Centre?
- Are there any parenting training programmes available, for example the fpa Speakeasy programme?

Tried and tested ideas

- Give parents a leaflet with **tips for talking to your child** about sex and relationships (see 'Introduction to SRE' leaflet towards the end of this publication). Include a tear-off section on the leaflet that parents can use, for example, to indicate their interest in participating in a workshop or listing topics that they want more help with.
- Produce a **list of books** that address sex and relationships topics that parents can read with their children. Make the books available to view at school and, if possible, to borrow. Liaise with the local library as they may be able to make these books available too.
- Include sessions on 'talking to your children about sex and relationships' as part of a **'carousel' of support meetings** for parents on different topics such as bullying and safety. Parents can discuss in pairs their 'Top Tips' for talking to their children and could also plan how they would answer 'awkward questions' from their children. (See programme for Varndean School awareness-raising meeting on page 11.)
- Workshops don't have to be just for parents. Plan **a joint parent-child event** on SRE. This can be an opportunity for children to showcase their work to parents in a safe environment and to enable parents and children to start talking to each other in a structured way (visit case study about Coten End Primary School on the Sex Education Forum website www.sexeducationforum.org.uk/practice/parents-sre).
- Run **short courses for parents** to build up knowledge and confidence to talk to their children about sex and relationships. These may be accredited courses such as the fpa Speakeasy course. Ensure the course tutor is sufficiently trained and supported. The course content

should be informed by the age and needs of the children and their parents. Integrating sessions on SRE into parenting courses offered by Sure Start and children's centres.

- Design a set of **worksheets that pupils take home** after an SRE lesson with a summary of what has been covered and suggestions for follow-up discussion topics at home. (This information can also be given to any parents who withdraw their children from SRE.)
- **Invite parents to view and help choose resources** prior to a particular topic being started in SRE, for example puberty. Discuss the criteria for selecting a resource with parents and demonstrate how the resource will be used so that the context is clear.

Case study: SRE book list for parents

BigTalk Education and North Lincolnshire Teenage Pregnancy Partnership have produced a recommended book list for parents and carers, children and teenagers covering topics to do with body science, sex and relationships. Young people from two school councils helped review the books and parents were also consulted about what to recommend. The book titles for younger children such as *Let's Talk* and *Boys, Girls & Body Science* are suitable for parents to read with their children. All the titles are available to borrow for free from local libraries and are stocked by local bookshops.

Primary schools have promoted the book list to parents and carers as part of an evening session about SRE that explains what the school will teach and how parents can support learning. Sessions run by BigTalk Education on 'Helping to keep your Children Safe' are also offered to parents at community and children's centres. The sessions cover how to talk to children about body science, relationships and sex, stressing the importance of starting to talk early in order to keep them safe.

Tips for involving parents in reviewing the choice of resources

Once parents have been invited to review the selection of resources the school wants to use, here are some tips on how to involve them in discussion.

- Start the meeting by explaining why the school has chosen this particular range of resources (for example, they are age appropriate, teachers are trained and comfortable using them, good feedback from pupils).
- Highlight why resources are important tools for teaching SRE and that visual resources are particularly important to help explain to children how the body works, anatomy and which parts of the body are private. This is very important learning that helps protect children from abuse. Show parents a selection of visual resources and discuss criteria for making a choice between them.
- Refer to the Sex Education Forum checklist for choosing and using resources, www.sexeducationforum.org.uk/resources

- Demonstrate how resources will be used within a lesson so that the context for using them is clear. A competent and skilful teacher is the best resource! Share video footage of an SRE lesson in which various resources have been used or share pupil work that responds to the resource.
- If parents are viewing resources either individually or in a group, invite feedback in a structured fashion. For example, lay out resources for parents to view then give parents a list of the resources and ask them to walk around and handle the resources and score each resource against criteria such as 'What messages about growing up or human reproduction does this resource give? Do these messages fit with the school's approach to SRE?', 'Does the resource show or talk about people in different family situations?' and 'Is this resource relevant to my child? Will they be interested in it?'.
- A small group of parents may want to get more involved in reviewing resources and perhaps developing a set of recommended books that parents can use at home with their children. This process can support parents to become more confident communicating about sex and relationships issues and thus more able to speak to their children at home. A full case study about how this approach has been used in Hillingdon is available from the 'Practice' section of the Sex Education Forum website (www.sexeducationforum.org.uk/practice/parents-sre).
- In some communities it may be more appropriate to invite parents to single sex sessions to review and discuss resources.

Case study collection

A sample of three case studies are provided below to show the range of ways in which parents can become actively involved in SRE and the benefits for children and families. Further case studies can be found under the theme 'Parents and SRE' in the Practice section of the Sex Education Forum website (www.sexeducationforum.org.uk/practice**).**

Case study: The 'Francly' programme

Schools and parents involved in a project exploring SRE resources said they would like more guidance on answering children's questions in an age-appropriate way. The 'Francly' programme has been developed in partnership with parents and staff at Charville Primary School in London Borough of Hillingdon. Francly stands for: Factual, Realistic, Affirmative/Age-appropriate, Non-judgmental, Continued, Learning in Younger years.

The programme aim was to develop a resource pack that supports teaching staff and parents on age-appropriate answers to children's questions related to SRE. Parents and teachers pooled their knowledge of common questions asked by children. Over the course of six meetings a group of parents and two school staff discussed age-appropriate answers to the questions. To inform their answers, participants looked at a timeline of normal sexual development of children and explored the pros and cons of talking about sensitive issues with children. Miriam Stoppard's book *Questions Children Ask* was used for inspiration and guidance. The questions and suggested answers will now be included in the school SRE policy and shared with other parents.

For further information contact Malin Stenstrom, email: *MStenstrom@ hillingdon.gov.uk*

Maria's experience of Speakeasy

This case study is written from the point of view of the Speakeasy facilitator, who is also a learning mentor coordinator. Names have been changed to protect privacy.

Maria is a single mum with four children ranging between 5 and 15 years old. I am a learning mentor coordinator and a trained Speakeasy facilitator. Maria came to see me initially about a year ago with concerns about the sexualised behaviour of her youngest son, to which she did not know how to respond. There had been some child protection concerns about neglect in the past. She told me that she feared her partner was sexually aggressive towards all her children and used inappropriate language. We undertook a Common Assessment Framework (CAF) with the family.

Maria told me that she finds it very hard to talk about sex and relationships and it is something she feels very uncomfortable with and would not want to talk about at all with anybody. I suggested she attend Speakeasy and she agreed.

At the first Speakeasy session Maria told the group that she had not spoken at all to either of her older children about puberty or any aspect of sex and relationships. It was simply something that was not mentioned in their house. Maria responded very well to being part of the group and to the way that Speakeasy works with learning together through discussion. She was extremely honest and open, as were other members of the group, and there was a strong sense of mutual support and respect among them from the first week, even though several of the parents did not know each other beforehand, and Maria did not know anyone as she is quite isolated socially where she lives.

At the start of the second session I asked for thoughts on the previous week's session. Maria told the group that she had sat down with her son and gone through the activity that we had done in the group. She had drawn the gingerbread figures on a piece of paper and together they had talked through and drawn or written on the changes that take place for boys during puberty. She said that it had been really successful and she had even managed to talk about wet dreams!

Maria attended every week. She borrowed the textbook and other books such as *Mummy Laid an Egg* and *Hair in Funny Places* by Babette Cole. She developed hugely in confidence throughout the weeks and in the final session she was quick to remember and answer key questions about what we had covered. She also expressed an interest in taking part in some 'protective behaviours' work and we have referred her for this.

The fpa Speakeasy programme offers a choice of accredited courses and shorter workshops for use with small groups of parents. It is designed to give parents confidence and knowledge to talk with their children about sex, relationships and growing up. More information can be found on the FPA website, www.fpa.org.uk/ communityprojects/parentsandcarers

Parents and Children Together (PACT) programme at Parc Eglos Primary School

The Parents and Children Together (PACT) programme was developed in Cornwall with the aim of developing partnerships between school and home, with a particular emphasis on children's personal development, aged 8–11, in relation to SRE. The programme is designed as a series of nine weekly one-hour sessions delivered by teachers in school. Parents receive weekly lesson plans about the curricula and children take home a 'family chat time' activity. Children and parents are encouraged to record their comments in a 'thought diary' throughout the programme.

Parc Eglos is a large primary school in Helston, Cornwall. Many of the 410 pupils on roll come from naval families. The school started using the PACT programme in 2006, and were particularly drawn to the SRE element of the programme. Parents proved to be generally very supportive of the programme aims. The built-in talk time activities completed the triangle of parent, child and teacher. This opened up discussions that previously might not have taken place outside the school building. Many parents reported that they had grown closer to their children and forged new bonds because of the link-up talking points they were sharing together.

The headteacher also devised a new way of delivering some of the lessons, inviting the parents of each year group into school once a term to share in the 'circle time' experience. Either the headteacher or the additional needs coordinator would lead what became known as 'PACT Assemblies', with pupils, parents, grandparents and other family members and carers taking part in a 40-minute version of the class lesson. In a cohort of 60 children an average of 20 adults attended.

The school has continued to develop SRE and PSHE and still works with PACT (soon to be known as 'Walk Tall'), SEAL, the Christopher Winter Project, Pyramid Club and other materials as they aim to address the changing social and emotional needs of their pupils.

Working with parents to support the needs of individual pupils

Communication between parents and school can be essential to supporting the needs of individual pupils. The personal nature of sex and relationships will raise particular issues for some children. Parents may need reassurance that SRE will reduce their child's vulnerability and increase their resilience.

Parents of pupils with special educational needs (SEN) may welcome additional support from school as they may be faced with behaviour from their child that is difficult to deal with, e.g. child approaching strangers to talk to them or touch them, revealing private parts of the body in public. Parents of children who have experienced sexual abuse or trauma are also likely to be concerned about how their child will cope with SRE. Parents may welcome the opportunity to discuss individual concerns with staff and develop common strategies to support the child or young person. For example, a parent with a child with gender identity issues may want their child to be given consistent messages at home and at school and may want to ensure that the school is doing work on gender stereotyping to help minimise the likelihood of their child being bullied.

To ensure a proactive approach schools can make it clear to parents that they are welcome to discuss the individual needs of their children for SRE. Issues affecting individual pupils can also arise during SRE lessons or the school day. For example if a pupil asks a question that the teacher feels would be useful for the parent to know about, a slip can be sent home stating:

> In SRE today your child asked about .... Please could you talk to your child about this at home. Let me know if you would like further help with this.

In some cases a question asked by a child in SRE may raise more serious concerns and this may prompt inviting the parent in for a discussion and/or following the school child protection protocol.

Care must be taken that any personal information about children is only shared with consent and only when necessary. For example, the HIV status of a child would not be information shared widely across the school community. It is good practice for a school to have a confidentiality policy and this can be cross-referenced to practice in SRE.

There may be times when the views of parents about how to best support their child in SRE are in conflict with the views of the school. A proactive and open dialogue is recommended that puts the needs of the child at the centre.

Involving specific groups of parents and carers

Schools are experienced in what type of communication works well for their parent community. It is important to make dialogue about SRE as inclusive as possible by using this know-how and also trying fresh approaches. Consider the themes and questions below to boost participation.

Language: Some parents will have limited literacy and/or speak English as an additional or second language. Do you need a translator? Is the choice of vocabulary as straightforward as possible? For example, Coombe Road Primary School in Brighton & Hove used the home school liaison worker from the Ethnic Minority Achievement Service to invite Bengali parents and carers to a meeting about the SRE policy and supported this consultation by translating for these parents at the meeting.

Technology: Text messaging, email and online communication have lots of benefits for communicating with parents. Are you using this technology to best advantage? How will you involve parents who can't access this technology?

Timing: Getting the time right will have a big impact on participation. Can you offer a meeting/activity at more than one time during the day/week? Do some parents need crèche facilities to be able to attend?

Place: Coming into school can be a big deal for some parents. Are there other venues where parents are more comfortable, for example the children's centre or a community venue?

Gender: Male and female carers are likely to engage in discussion about SRE in different ways and this will have a cultural and/or religious dimension too. Talk to parents to understand what they will be comfortable with and consider running separate events for men and women. For example, if the majority of parents taking part in a Speakeasy course are female, the school may consider running a separate course exclusively for men.

Religion and belief: Awareness of the faith background of families will help ensure that parents and carers are able to engage in dialogue about SRE.

Information for schools working with parents and carers of Looked After Children in relation to SRE

Looked After Children are more likely to have experienced trauma relating to personal and family relationships. They may also have less opportunity to discuss growing up, sex and relationships with their family members. So it is important that their carers can offer them support in this area.

The Children Act 1989 emphasises the importance of working in partnership with parents on all matters concerning the upbringing of a Looked After Child. This includes informing parents about how issues relating to personal relationships and sexual health will be addressed.

Some local authorities have developed SRE and sexual health guidance specifically for working with Looked After Children. Local guidance and practice varies, but there are some consistent principles:

- there should be dialogue with parents or those with parental responsibility about what SRE is provided for a child.
- the best interest of the child must be considered, for example in cases where a parent is reluctant to allow their child SRE.
- parental engagement with SRE provided in the school attended by a Looked After Child becomes a joint involvement of the local authority/carers and parents/those with parental responsibility.

A Looked After Child may have missed out on SRE taught in school, so it is really important that school and carers work together to ensure the child gets the full support and information they need.

Involving the wider community in SRE

The knowledge, values and experience held in the communities in which children and young people live are a rich resource that can contribute to SRE. Parents and carers are part of the local community, as are faith and cultural leaders, voluntary and community organisations, health services and other specialised professionals. Faith and cultural beliefs have an important role in shaping children and young people's views and decisions about sex and relationships. It is helpful, therefore, that faith and cultural perspectives are acknowledged and explored within SRE.

Knowledge of the local community and needs assessment carried out with pupils will identify particular local issues relevant to SRE, such as high incidence of HIV, teenage pregnancy, domestic violence, forced marriage and female genital mutilation. Schools may find there are local community resources such as voluntary organisations to help them with these issues. Schools must also be clear about the law, for example, forced marriage and female genital mutilation are illegal.

Specialised voluntary sector organisations and cultural groups within the community may be able to help by training local teachers so that they can develop a curriculum that better meets local needs. They may also offer to work directly with pupils. Visitor input can enrich SRE when carefully selected, well managed and properly integrated within the curriculum. The Sex Education Forum has produced a guide to working with external visitors, which can be downloaded from www.sexeducationforum.org.uk/schools/community-engagement

Children and young people have said that discussing the faith and values perspectives of their families and communities openly and positively is important to them and they want this to be part of SRE. A skilled teacher will be able to plan activities that are relevant to young people and draw on the cultural life of the local community. Local authorities should ensure that SRE training provided locally for teachers and governors reflects issues that are of concern to the local community.

The Sex Education Forum book *Religion and Belief* (yet to be published) provides practical advice for developing dialogue on SRE with parents and other community members.

Case study: Engaging with parents in Nottingham
The Nottingham Healthy Schools Team recruited an SRE advisor to work specifically with Asian members of the community to support parents and community members to understand the SRE programme in schools. The SRE advisor runs consultation sessions for parents explaining how SRE fits with culture and faith, especially Islam, since 80 per cent of Asian secondary students identified themselves as Muslim in a survey carried out by the Healthy Schools Team. The consultations begin at primary school level and are offered in both single sex and mixed sex settings. Often fathers/mothers attending the single sex sessions go home and talk to each other and then provide their feedback to the school. The SRE advisor invites a range of local community and school staff to support this process. This can include Asian language speakers to help translate, teaching assistants, governors and local community members.

Consulting and engaging with parents at primary school level is proving to be a good foundation for better understanding and support for SRE at secondary level as children progress through schooling. The SRE advisor has also developed teachers' confidence in creating policy, schemes of work and delivering SRE that is inclusive of the Asian community.

What if ...

These three scenarios provide some guidance for schools about how to handle some potentially difficult situations in relation to parents and SRE.

What if a parent meets you to request that their child be withdrawn from SRE, complaining that schools are sexualising their children by teaching them how to have sex?

- Thank the parent for coming to talk to you and for taking SRE seriously.
- Ask the parent if there is anything in particular that has made them concerned that the SRE at the school is sexualising their children.
- Explain that all teaching in SRE encourages pupils to think carefully about sexual relationships and does not encourage them to have sex.
- Explain that researchers have studied the effects of SRE and found that it does not make young people have sex. In fact, it has the opposite effect since young people who have had good SRE have sexual intercourse for the first time at an older age.
- Talk to the parent about other influences that may be a worry, such as the internet and images in advertising. Explain that in SRE lessons the myths and misinformation that are sometimes spread between friends and from the internet are challenged and correct facts are given to pupils.
- Ask the parent if they want any more information about the SRE curriculum and resources used.

NB: Parents do not have to give the school reasons for exercising their right of withdrawal.

What if a group of parents write a letter asking that all teaching about homosexuality be removed from the curriculum?

- Invite the parents to meet with you to discuss the letter.
- Explain to the parents that the law states that schools must promote equal opportunities and must challenge discrimination relating to sexual orientation and also gender.
- Explain that the school has an inclusive curriculum, so same-sex relationships are mentioned along with opposite-sex relationships and both marriage and civil partnerships are covered. Show parents an example of how this might happen in a lesson in practice.
- Show the parents the SRE policy that sets out the school's aims for SRE and the values on which it rests and explain how parents are involved in its production.
- Ask the parents if there is any particular lesson or activity in the school that has caused them to be concerned.
- Show parents how the issue of sexual orientation is handled in the curriculum. For example, show common questions asked by pupils such as 'What does gay mean?' and demonstrate how these questions are answered.
- Invite parents to speak with you individually after the meeting.

What if a parent asks that their child be withdrawn from accessing the on-site sexual health services?

- Tell the parent that the health services available at school are just the same as health services outside the school and young people (of any age) are free to see a nurse or doctor by themselves.
- Reassure the parent that just like health services outside school, the same measures are in place to protect young people. This means that a nurse or doctor will always encourage a young person to talk to their parents about the problem for which they are seeking advice.
- Explain to the parent that pupils use the health facility at school for a wide range of issues, for example questions about periods, growing up and friendships. A small percentage of (mostly) older pupils seek sexual health advice from this service.
- Tell the parent that the fact pupils are having SRE will help protect them, and young people who have good SRE are more likely to be older when they first have sexual intercourse. Explain that pupils also learn about the wide range of topics they can seek help for at the health centre.
- Offer to give the parent a guided tour of the health facilities on the school site.

Key resources

SRE resource list for parents and carers produced by the Sex Education Forum: www.sexeducationforum.org.uk/resources/resources-for-sre	Parents and SRE (Sex Education Forum 2011); an accessible summary of the research evidence: www.sexeducationforum.org.uk/evidence	Case studies providing examples of how schools around the country are involving parents and carers in SRE: www.sexeducationforum.org.uk/practice/parents-sre	Speakeasy programme run by the fpa: *www.fpa.org.uk/communityprojects/parentsandcarers*
Family Lives provides information and advice to families on a wide range of topics including risky behaviour and growing up: www.familylives.org.uk	'Talking to Your Teenager about Sex and Relationships', a leaflet for parents of teenagers produced by NHS and Parentline (2009): https://www.education.gov.uk/publications/standard/Youthandadolescence/Page3/DCSF-00605-2009)	NHS website with information for parents about puberty: www.nhs.uk/Livewell/puberty/Pages/Pubertyinfoforparents.aspx	Advice on internet safety from the Child Exploitation and Online Protection (CEOP) Centre, in particular the 'thinkuknow' site for parents: https://www.thinkuknow.co.uk/parents/

The activities

Part 1: Multimedia survey activities

These survey style activities can be integrated into other communications for parents, for example communications about PSHE as a whole or other aspects of school life such as equalities or bullying. Data from these surveys will provide important evidence to Ofsted about how the school works in partnership with parents and how parental views are collected and used.

Activity 1: Quick audit questions

Activity 2: Annual audit questions

Part 2: Activities for face-to-face meetings and workshops

Activities in this section are designed for use when meeting with parents face to face, for example in a workshop or parents' evening.

Activity 3: Working agreement

Activity 4: What is SRE? Values and content

Activity 5: Reviewing parents' own experience of SRE

Activity 6: The unique role of parents in SRE

Activity 7: The best parent educator

Activity 1: Quick audit questions

Purpose
To raise awareness about SRE in the school and initiate further parental involvement.

Outcomes
By carrying out this survey:

- parents and schools will have entered into a basic dialogue about SRE
- the school will have benchmark data about parents' awareness and involvement.

Notes to facilitator
These questions could be communicated through a virtual learning environment (VLE), text message, website survey tool or on paper. The advantage of using an electronic tool such as a web-based survey is that the responses can be counted automatically. Explain to parents why you want their views and what you intend to do with them. Keep a record of how many parents respond and their answers.

The questions

- Did you know there is a school policy on sex and relationships education (SRE)?

  Yes   /   No   /   Not sure

- Has your child ever talked to you about something they learnt at school to do with growing up, sex and relationships?

  Yes   /   No   /   Not sure

- Has your child ever asked you questions about growing up, sex and relationships?

  Yes   /   No   /   Not sure

- Would you like more information about what the school teaches on sex and relationships?

  Yes   /   No   /   Maybe

- Do you want more support to help you talk to your child about sex and relationships issues at home?

  Yes   /   No   /   Not sure

Activity 2: Annual audit questions

Purpose
To find out how engaged parents are with SRE in the school and to track changes in this year on year.

Outcomes
By carrying out this survey:

- parents will have reflected on their communications with school and their child(ren) relating to SRE over the last year
- the school can see if parental engagement on SRE has changed compared to previous years
- the school has a measure of how parents rate SRE provision.

Notes to facilitator
By asking parents for more information about themselves, data from the audit can be disaggregated. For example, you may find differences in how males and females respond to the questions. When contacting parents explain why you are carrying out the survey and how the data will be used.

The questions

About you:

- Are you?

  Male   /   Female

- Which school years are your children in?

  Year 1 / 2 / 3 / 4 / 5 / 6

  Year 7 / 8 / 9 / 10 / 11

In the last year:

- Have you read the school SRE policy?

  Yes   /   No   /   Part of it   /   Not sure

- Has your child spoken to you about an SRE lesson at school or shown you work that they have done in an SRE lesson?

  Yes   /   No   /   Not sure

- If yes, did you feel able to talk about it further with your child?

  Yes   /   No   /   Not sure

- As a parent, do you feel you have made a positive contribution to your child's SRE this year?

  Yes   /   No   /   Not sure

- Have you discussed SRE with a teacher or staff member at school?

  Yes   /   No   /   Can't remember

- Do you feel the school has involved you enough with discussions about SRE?

  Yes   /   No   /   Not sure

Based on your experiences over the past year, how would you describe the SRE provision at this school?

  Very good   /   Good   /   OK   /   Bad   /   Very bad

What are your suggestions for improvement?

_____

_____

Activity 3: Working agreement

Before starting any group activities with parents, it is essential to make an agreement about how people will work together. This helps a group to feel safe to talk about SRE.

Purpose
To establish a climate that enables people to work together confidently.

Outcome
By the end of this activity parents will have agreed on specific behaviours that they will adopt for the duration of the workshop or meeting.

Materials
Flipchart paper
Marker pens

Time
10–15 minutes

Activity

- Ask the group to discuss in pairs what will help them to feel comfortable talking as a group about SRE.

- Encourage people to think of specific behaviours, such as 'no interrupting', 'not disclosing personal information'.

- Write up contributions on a flipchart to ensure clarity, shared understanding and agreement.

- Ensure that the agreement is visible to all participants throughout the workshop.

Activity 4: What is SRE?
Values and content

Purpose
To ensure that parents have an understanding that is shared with the school of what sex and relationships education is.

Outcomes
By the end of this activity parents will be able to list:

• topics that can be included in SRE
• values that underpin SRE.

Materials
Paper or sticky notes
Coloured pens
The school SRE policy

Time
30 minutes +

Activity

• Explain to parents that the title 'SRE' can be confusing and that you want to make sure everyone knows what is meant by it. You can add that SRE has different names in different schools and is sometimes just called 'sex education' as a kind of shorthand.

• Check that parents know that 'SRE' stands for 'sex and relationships education'.

• Point out that the word 'sex' has a wide meaning in the English language – it doesn't just mean sexual intercourse. 'Sex' also indicates biological sex as in 'girl' or 'boy', thus the question 'What is the sex of the baby?'.

• Present parents with the broad topic headings covered in SRE. Suggested headings used within the Sex Education Forum curriculum design tool are: Relationships, My body, Feelings and attitudes, Life cycles and human reproduction, Keeping safe and looking after myself, Getting advice and help.

• Ask parents to work in pairs or small groups and brainstorm the topics that they think should be covered under each of these headings. Parents may be concerned about what topics should be introduced at what age group. For the purposes of this activity, ask parents to think about what should be covered by the time a child leaves primary or secondary school. Ideas can be written on sticky notes or directly onto a large piece of paper. To save time you can distribute the headings so that each pair or group works on one or two headings.

- Give parents time to look at what others have suggested. Ask 'Is there anything on the list that surprises you?', 'Is there anything on the list that you think shouldn't be included?', 'Is there anything still missing?'. To avoid getting stuck on any one topic, use different coloured pens to mark and record topics that people comment on. These comments can be revisited individually after the session or on another occasion.

- Now introduce the idea of values using examples of the school values. Ask the group to consider what values are needed to teach the SRE topics they have listed. Make a list of values proposed by the group. Prompt for core values such as love, care, respect and valuing diversity. Refer back to individual topics and ask the group 'What values are needed when teaching children about puberty?' for example.

- There are likely to be core values that participants agreed on and then there may be more personal values that are not universally shared. Draw attention to the core values. Share information from the school SRE policy that relates to values. Ask parents if anything is missing from the policy relating to values that can be added. Encourage parents to communicate their more personal family values relating to sex and relationships directly to their children at home.

- To extend the activity parents can brainstorm the type of skills they think their children can develop through SRE.

Activity 5: Reviewing parents' own experience of SRE

Purpose

To relate parents' own experiences of SRE to what they want for their children.

Outcomes

By the end of this activity parents will have:

- recalled both positive and negative experiences of their own SRE at home and school
- identified the qualities of SRE they want to shape the SRE their children receive.

Notes to facilitator

This activity can be used to generate a framework for reviewing the school SRE policy or simply to get parents thinking about what they want for their children.

Fathers and male carers often have had poorer experiences of SRE than mothers and female carers. Look for an opportunity to tactfully discuss such variation and point out that research shows that fathers are less likely than mothers to talk to their children about sex and relationships.

Materials

For the facilitator: Flipchart/board
For the parents: Paper and pen

Time

40 minutes

Activity

- First revisit the working agreement and emphasise that participants are free to choose what and how much they share.

- The facilitator can begin by recalling their own experience of SRE for example:

  My experience of SRE at school was very limited. In primary school the girls had a talk about periods and the boys went for extra sport and heard a bit about it when the girls chatted afterwards in the playground. I learnt more at home because my parents bought me a book about puberty but I don't think we ever talked about it.

- Ask parents to work in pairs and try to remember their own experience of learning about sex and relationships as a child. Pose questions 1–4 on the board or flipchart. Keep question 6 covered.

  1 What topics did you learn about at school?

  2 What was discussed at home?

3 Did you learn from other places apart from home and school?

4 What was good about how it was taught / discussed at school / home / anywhere else?

5 What was bad about how it was taught / discussed at school / home / anywhere else?

6 What do you want to be the same or different for your own child's SRE?

- After 10 minutes collect brief feedback from the pairs. For example, ask pairs to decide if they learnt more from home or school. Parents can raise their hands as a group to show their response. The facilitator notes any common themes.

- Return to work in pairs to discuss question 6: 'What do you want to be the same or different for your own child's SRE'? (10 mins). Ask pairs to write down a minimum of three statements starting 'I want my child's SRE to be …'.

- Pairs feed back their statements to the plenary and the facilitator records points on the flipchart or board. The facilitator can group similar points together. Where points contradict mention that parents will differ in what they want for their children's SRE. Encourage parents to see the activity as a chance to reflect on how they personally want to support their children and also a chance to find out how other parents feel.

- To extend this activity, use ideas generated from question 6 as a framework for reviewing the school SRE policy. The facilitator will need to work with the group to identify points on which there is general agreement. Take each point at a time and see if this is supported by the existing policy and, if not, how the policy could be changed.

Activity 6: The unique role of parents in SRE

Purpose

To appreciate the different and mutually supportive roles that parents and schools can have in a child's SRE.

Outcomes

By the end of this activity parents can:

- identify some unique qualities that parents have in providing SRE
- identify some unique qualities that schools have in providing SRE
- find ways in which school and parents can support each other with SRE.

Notes to facilitator

Parents need to have explored definitions of SRE prior to this activity, for example using Activity 3.

Materials

Parents: Pieces of flipchart paper and marker pens
Facilitator: Flipchart with the heading 'The unique role of parents in SRE' and another piece with 'The unique role of schools in SRE'. For a big group prepare several.

Time

20–30 minutes

Activity

- Introduce the activity by asking parents to think of all the different people and places or information sources that children get information about sex and relationships from. Ask people to share their ideas with a partner.

- Ask pairs to report back if they thought of 'home' and 'school'. What else did they think of? Point out that home and school are both places where children can get safe and reliable information from adults.

- Now explain that national surveys (or a school survey if you have done one) have found that children want SRE from both school and home. National (or local) surveys also show that most parents think there is a role for themselves and also the school with SRE. For example, in a survey by Mumsnet (2011) 98 per cent of parents said that they are happy for their children to attend school SRE lessons.

- Pose the question 'What makes SRE at home and school different or are they the same?' Gather a few responses from the group.

- Now divide participants into small groups of three to six people. Ask groups to spend 10 minutes brainstorming under the headings pre-written on the flipchart. Ask half the groups to start by thinking about 'what is unique about SRE that parents provide' and half about 'what is unique about SRE that schools provide'.

- Ask groups to swap flipcharts so that each group looks at the other topic and has the chance to add further points.

- If there are lots of groups, ask parents to walk around and look at all the work.

- The activity can be finished at this point by acknowledging that both school and home have complementary roles in SRE.

- To extend the activity, explore ways in which school and home can work together. Ask groups to pair up thus making double-sized groups. Focus on the lists for the unique role of parents. Ask the groups to think of things that make it difficult for parents to fulfil their role with SRE. These points can be written directly on the flipchart as a record. Now return to the plenary and ask for ideas about how these difficulties can be overcome and what role the school can play in this.

Activity 7: The best parent educator

Purpose
To learn about effective educational strategies that parents can use informally for SRE at home.

Outcomes
By the end of this activity participants will be:

- familiar with the educational strategies that parents can use for SRE at home
- able to put some of these strategies into place in a real situation.

Notes to facilitator
This activity can be used with parents or as part of training for professionals that support parents such as parent liaison officers and SRE teachers. This activity builds well from Activity 6: The unique role of parents in SRE.

Materials
Facilitator: copies of case study, copies of Walker's list of assets.

Activity

- Introduce the activity by giving this background information:

  Researchers have asked children and parents what they think makes a good parent educator on SRE. Most children wanted their parents to avoid seeing SRE as a one-off event or 'the big talk'. Instead they thought SRE should be an ongoing process. Thinking of SRE in this way can help reduce anxiety for parents and means discussions can grow as a child develops.

  Parents have also said they are unsure if they should initiate conversations about sex and relationships or just respond to a child's questions. Another dilemma for parents is how open they should be, while also respecting the need for privacy.

- Ask parents to discuss in pairs the following statement and decide if they agree or disagree with it: 'When they're old enough to ask, they're old enough to know'.

- Pairs feed back to the plenary. The facilitator asks parents to consider if this approach is used for other things we learn about, such as how to cross the road, healthy eating and being a good friend. This discussion will probably reveal some dilemmas about how best to educate children.

- Introduce the list of educational strategies (see Communication Techniques Used by Parents on next page) that a researcher (Walker 2001) found are used by parents when they are confident in their role as sex and relationships educators.

- Now ask parents to work in pairs (mix the pairs up if parents are comfortable together). Each pair begins looking at one scenario and should pick a minimum of three of Walker's educational strategies in their response. Spread the four different scenarios between the pairs.

- If you have time this activity can be developed into a role-play. Two volunteers play out the scenario and the other participants note which educational strategies are used by the parent.

Communication Techniques Used by Parents

being available

being approachable

being supportive

revisiting topics

using intuition

employing humour

giving unconditional respect

being open and honest

listening

checking out understanding

Adapted from Walker, JL (2001) 'A qualitative study of parents' experiences of providing sex education for their children: The implications for health education'.

Case study scenarios

1 Your daughter comes home from primary school upset and tells you about an incident in the playground where she was teased about having big breasts.

   What will you, the parent, do? Can you use at least three of Walker's educational strategies?

   Circle the three strategies you will use and explain what you will do.

2 Your son comes home from secondary school (Year 7) upset and tells you about a bullying incident. A group of older pupils had been sending him inappropriate text messages with sexual content.

   What will you, the parent, do? Can you use at least three of Walker's educational strategies?

   Circle the three strategies you will use and explain what you will do.

3 A story about a young girl being raped is on the TV news. You are watching with your 14-year-old son.

   What will you, the parent, do? Can you use at least three of Walker's educational strategies?

   Circle the three strategies you will use and explain what you will do.

4 While out shopping with your daughter, you hear a group of young people bullying a boy telling him he is 'so gay'.

   What will you, the parent, do? Can you use at least three of Walker's educational strategies?

   Circle the three strategies you will use and explain what you will do.

5 Your son asks your permission to attend an all-night party at a friend's house.

   What will you, the parent, do? Can you use at least three of Walker's educational strategies?

   Circle the three strategies you will use and explain what you will do.

Sample letter for parent choosing to withdraw child from SRE

Dear _ _ _ _ _ _ _ _ _ _ _ _ _ _ _ _ _

Thank you for your letter about _

You do have the right to withdraw your son/daughter from the sex and relationships education provided in addition to National Curriculum Science in school. I completely understand that you wish your son/ daughter to have the cultural/religious context to relationships and sex within marriage that belongs to your family.

I'm very glad to hear that you take this matter seriously at home – I only wish all parents would talk to their children about their family values for relationships.

There are a few things that I would like to share with you, and perhaps you will think about them.

- Firstly, sex and relationships education is taught with the clear understanding that accurate information will help young people as they grow up and prepare for adulthood. We are fully trained to give them accurate information.
- We do encourage young people to wait until they are certain they are ready before becoming sexually intimate with someone, and we also teach that some young people will choose to wait until they are married.
- It is likely that your child will hear about the lessons from classmates, and sometimes the information that they share may be only part of the facts. We always encourage young people to ask questions to make sure they have got their facts right in the lesson.
- We know that young people get incorrect information and myths about relationships and sex from their friends as well as media including the internet. Some of this information is inaccurate and in fact pretty damaging and crude. In our lessons, we are careful to always challenge disrespectful language and views and point out how media can be misleading.

We appreciate very much and have the utmost respect for religious and cultural views about these matters. We also know that children are growing up in a world that does not always share those values. We think it is important that all children have the opportunity to understand other points of view, and indeed to share their own important views.

I think it would be excellent if your son/daughter were in these lessons so that other students could hear his/her point of view. It would add to the information that you are sharing with him/her at home, and help him/her on his/her journey to becoming a well-informed and educated young man/woman.

I hope you will feel reassured by this information and decide that your son/daughter can attend the SRE lessons. If you do decide to withdraw your child, then I will be happy to discuss ways in which school can support you in fulfilling your role as educators at home.

Please come and see me at school to discuss this further or complete the form below.

With regards

Name

Role

I, parent of _ _ _ _ _ _ _ _ _ _ _ would like to arrange a meeting with the Head of SRE on _ _ _ _ _ _ _ _ date.

I, parent of _ _ _ _ _ _ _ _ _ _ _ would like to withdraw my child from the SRE lessons provided in addition to National Curriculum Science by the school until further notice.

I, parent of _ _ _ _ _ _ _ _ _ _ _ _ would like my child to attend the SRE lessons provided in addition to National Curriculum Science.

This letter is adapted from material developed by secondary school teacher Boo Spurgeon.

An introduction to SRE for parents and carers of primary school children

What is SRE?

Sex and relationships education (SRE) is learning about growing up, relationships, sexual health and reproduction. This includes:

- **physical** development, for example how our bodies change in puberty
- **emotions**, like how to manage feelings, and
- the **social** side of it, such as positive and negative influences from friends.

SRE gives children and young people essential knowledge to help them stay safe and understand what is happening as they grow up.

Whatever topic children are learning about in SRE, teaching should always stress the values of love, respect and care for one another.

Why is SRE important?

Puberty and growing up is a normal part of life but something that many adults find difficult to talk about. Adult embarrassment can stop children getting honest answers to their questions. Because of this many children go through puberty without a basic understanding about how their bodies work.

Children get information about sex and relationships from other sources such as the internet, adverts, newspapers, magazines, television and friends. But a lot of this is unreliable and misleading. Children will still get this jumble of information, which is sometimes very frightening, even if no-one at home or school talks about sex and relationships.

Children need to get reliable information about growing up, having babies and staying safe, from both their school and family.

When should SRE start?

SRE needs to start early in primary school so that children learn about their bodies, can recognise if other people make them feel uncomfortable or unsafe and can report abuse and get help. Lots of children start puberty before they leave primary school so it is important that all pupils know what to expect before it happens.

It is good to have some SRE in every year of primary school as it helps to learn a bit at a time and get more detail gradually as children mature.

Is there any evidence that SRE works?

National and international research shows that young people who have good SRE are more likely to be older when they have sex for the first time, to have fewer sexual partners and to use contraception. There is no evidence that teaching children about sex and relationships encourages them to have sex.

All parents and professionals want young people to wait until they are ready to have sex. This message is taught in all good quality SRE. For some young people, this may not be until they get married or enter into a civil partnership.

What can I expect from my child's school?

It is compulsory for primary schools to teach about human life cycles as part of science. But good SRE includes much more than just the biological basics. Each school must choose what it will teach about relationships and how to do this.

Schools must have an SRE policy and parents have the right to see the policy. This will state what the school teaches about sex and relationships (in addition to science). Academies and free schools can choose to have an SRE policy.

As a parent or carer you can expect to be asked for your views on SRE in the school. You may have suggestions to make about what topics need to be covered. Based on your knowledge of your child, you may also feel that some topics are being taught too late. For example, introducing puberty in Year 6 may be too late.

The school is likely to inform you about your right to opt your child out of SRE lessons (but not the teaching covered in science). If you have questions about this do talk to the school as often parents are reassured once they have spoken privately to the teacher.

What can I do at home?

Children say that they want their parents to be the first to talk to them about growing up, sex and relationships. So there is a lot you can do at home. Many parents want to do this but find it embarrassing and difficult. Try using the tips below to get started and have a look at the guide to what children want to learn about at different ages.

Tips for talking to your child about growing up, sex and relationships

Do

- Read books, leaflets, look at a website or watch a DVD with your child.
- Talk while you're doing something else – washing up, driving in the car, fishing or going for a walk.
- Enjoy talking about it. Laugh with each other, not at each other – it can reduce embarrassment and stress.

- Listen rather than judge. Try asking what your child thinks. Make sure you understand what your child's question really is. It may be much simpler than it first sounds.
- Answer questions and don't be afraid to say: 'I really don't know – let's work it out or look it up together'.
- Have a phrase ready for awkward moments, such as: 'That's a good question, let's talk about it once we get home' (then make sure you do).
- Always respond, if you don't, she or he may think it is wrong to talk to you about sex and relationships and as a result you may find your child clams up when you raise the subject.
- If it all feels too personal, try talking about people in books, films, and favourite television programmes such as soaps.

Don't

- Say you will tell them when they are older if they ask a question about sex. Instead, find a way to answer them that matches their level of understanding. If you don't know the answer, look at how you can find out together, for example on the internet.
- Bombard your child with questions if they ask you a question. If you are concerned about a question or a comment they have made, gently try to find out why they are asking it. Do try and hold on to your anxieties until you have a better idea of the origins of the question.
- Talk too much. Children say it is awful to get a lecture on growing up. Try to make it a two-way conversation.
- Be afraid to tell your children what you think, and why. But do try and avoid making harsh judgements of others and give your child some leeway to come to their own opinions.

 # What do children want to learn about at different ages?

Age 3–6
At this age children are interested in the differences between boys and girls, naming body parts, where babies come from, and friends and family. What areas of the body are private and should not be touched and who they can talk to if they are worried are also important.

Age 7–8
At this age children are interested in the emotional and physical changes of growing up, similarities and differences between boys and girls, coping with strong emotions and how babies are made from eggs and sperm. How to look after our bodies and how to be safe and healthy are also important.

Age 9–10
At this age children are interested in knowing about love and the different kinds of families. They will be curious about puberty and sexual feelings and changing body image. They will want more details about conception, how babies develop and are born and why families are important for having babies.

They will also be interested in knowing about how people can get diseases, including HIV, from sex and how they can be prevented. They will also want to know who they can talk to if they want help or advice and information about growing up.

Examples of how you can answer your child's questions

Answers to questions should be the continuation of a conversation not a speech ending in a full stop! So you might need to ask your child more questions to make sure they have understood and that you have understood them at their level. For each question have a look at the suggestions about what you might want to include in your discussion.

Child age 3–6: Why are girls and boys bodies different?

That's an interesting question. The reason is that girls grow up to be women and a woman's body can grow a baby inside it. Boys grow up to be men. Men can be fathers but the baby doesn't grow inside the father's body. So woman and men need different bodies so that they can make babies. Do you think there is anything else that makes a girl's and boy's body different?

Child age 7–8: What are eggs and sperm?

They are found inside our bodies. Eggs are inside a woman's body and sperm are inside a man's body. Human eggs and sperm are very tiny and too small to see. To make a baby there needs to be one egg and one sperm and they need to join together. Then they can grow into a baby inside the woman's body. Do you know where the eggs and sperm are stored?

Child age 9–10: Can people of the same sex love each other?

That's a very good thing to ask. Yes, two women or two men can love each other. It is just the same as when a man and woman love each other. The feelings are the same.

For more help and advice

- Ask your child's school how they are supporting parents with SRE
- Visit the Family Lives website www.familylives.org.uk
- Visit this NHS website with information for parents about puberty www. nhs.uk/Livewell/puberty/Pages/Pubertyinfoforparents.aspx
- For advice on internet safety visit the CEOP 'thinkuknow' site for parents https://www.thinkuknow.co.uk/parents/

An introduction to SRE for parents and carers of children at secondary school

What is SRE?

Sex and relationships education (SRE) is learning about growing up, relationships, reproduction and sexual health. This includes:

- **physical** development, for example how our reproductive systems work,
- **emotions**, like how to manage feelings, and
- the **social** side of it, such as positive and negative influences from friends.

SRE gives young people essential knowledge to help them stay safe and understand what is happening as they grow up.

Whatever topic young people learn about in SRE, teaching should always stress the values of love, respect and care for one another.

Why is SRE important?

Growing up and sexual development is a normal part of life but many people find it difficult to talk about. Adult embarrassment can stop young people getting honest answers to their questions. As a result many young people go through adolescence without a basic understanding about how their bodies work and without talking to an adult they trust about things such as what is important in intimate relationships.

The teenage years can be an exciting time but there are difficult things too like changes in friendships, changes in hormones and emotions and forming an adult identity.

Young people come across information about sex and relationship on the internet, in newspapers, magazines, adverts, film, television and from talking to friends. Sometimes this will happen by accident, such as finding sexual images through the internet on a mobile phone. Young people will still get this jumble of information, which is sometimes very frightening, even if no-one at home or schools talks about sex and relationships.

Young people need to get reliable information about healthy sexual development and how to stay safe from both school and their family.

What is taught at what age?

SRE should have started in primary school so that children are prepared for growing up and have learnt about how to stay safe. Teaching in secondary school should build on this knowledge.

Age 11–13
Most young people will be going through puberty and will be interested in hormones, how they will be affected by them, the menstrual cycle, wet

Let's work together

dreams, erections, fertility, pregnancy – how it can be avoided, and safer sex. They may also be wondering if their physical development is 'normal'.

Young teens also want to know about the difference between sexual attraction and love and whether it is usual to be attracted or in love with someone of the same gender. Young people will be asking questions about relationships, when is the right time to have sex, how to avoid pressure and where they can get more information if they need it, including the best websites.

Age 14–16

At this age young people want to know about different types of relationships. They may want to know about how to cope with strong feelings and how to cope with the pressures to have sex. They will be interested to know what they should expect of a partner and how to talk to them. They will need more information on contraception, sexual health and how to access services. They may ask questions about parenthood and may like to know how they can talk to their own parents or a trusted adult.

Most young people will not have sexual intercourse until they are at least 16 but statistics show that about a quarter of young people will have had sexual intercourse by the time they are 16.

Is there any evidence that SRE works?

National and international research shows that young people who have good SRE are more likely to choose to have sex for the first time when they are older, to have fewer sexual partners and to use contraception. There is no evidence that teaching young people about sex and relationships encourages them to have sex.

All parents and professionals want young people to wait until they are ready to have sex. This message is taught in all good quality SRE. For some young people, this may not be until they get married or enter into a civil partnership.

What can I expect from my child's school?

It is compulsory for secondary schools to teach about human reproduction as part of science and also to have a sex education programme that includes learning about HIV and other STIs. Good SRE includes much more than just the biological basics. Each school must choose what it will teach about relationships and how to do this.

Schools must have a SRE policy and parents have the right to see the policy. This will state what the school teaches about sex and relationships (in addition to science). Academies and free schools can choose to have an SRE policy.

As a parent or carer you can expect to be asked for your views on SRE in the school. You may have suggestions to make about what topics need to be covered.

The school is likely to inform you about your right to opt your child out of SRE lessons (but not the teaching covered in science). If you have questions about this do talk to the school as often parents are reassured once they have spoken privately to the teacher.

What can I do at home?

Young people say that they want their parents to be the first to talk to them about growing up, sex and relationships. You may feel you have missed opportunities when your children were younger to talk to them about growing up. It is not too late, but bear in mind that teens will want to keep some things private. Many parents put off talking to their children because they find it embarrassing and awkward.

Try using the tips below to get started and have a look at the guide to what young people want to learn about at different ages.

Tips for talking to your child about growing up, sex and relationships

Do

- Read books and leaflets, look at a website or watch a DVD with your child.
- Talk while you're doing something else – washing up, driving in the car, fishing or going for a walk.
- Enjoy talking about it. Laugh with each other, not at each other – it can reduce embarrassment and stress.
- Listen rather than judge. Try asking what your child thinks.
- Answer questions and don't be afraid to say: 'I really don't know – let's work it out or look it up together'.
- Have a phrase ready for awkward moments, such as: 'That's a good question, let's talk about it once we get home' (then make sure you do).
- Always respond, if you don't, she or he may think it is wrong to talk to you about sex and relationships and as a result you may find your child clams up when you raise the subject.
- If it all feels too personal, try talking about people in books, films, and favourite television programmes such as soaps.

Don't

- Bombard your child with questions or talk too much. Many young people say it is awful to get the big lecture on sex or questions fired at them – 'I asked a question and she immediately came back with "Are you having sex then?"' Try and hold on to your anxieties, answer the question, and respect privacy. Young people go through phases of wanting to be private. Let them know you are happy to talk to them whenever they are ready.
- Be afraid to tell your children what you think, and why. It's also helpful to recognise that other people they know may have different opinions. Asking your child's opinion shows them that you are interested in what they think and might make them feel less anxious about talking to you.

For more help and advice

- Ask your child's school how they are supporting parents with SRE
- Visit Family Lives www.familylives.org.uk
- Visit this NHS website with information for parents about puberty www.nhs.uk/Livewell/puberty/Pages/Pubertyinfoforparents.aspx
- For advice on internet safety visit the CEOP 'thinkuknow' site for parents https://www.thinkuknow.co.uk/parents/

References

Department for Education and Employment (2000) *Sex and Relationships Education Guidance for Schools.* London: DfEE.

Desforges, C and Abouchaar, A (2003) *The Impact of Parental Involvement, Parental Support and Family Education On Pupil Achievement and Adjustment: A Literature Review,* DfES.

Durex, NAHT, NCPTA, NGA (2010) *Sex and Relationship Education: Views from teachers, parents and governors.* http://www.durexhcp.co.uk/downloads/SRE-report.pdf (accessed 20 November 2012).

General Teaching Council (2006) Research for teachers; Parental involvement, GTC. Available from http://www.tla.ac.uk/site/SiteAssets/RfT1/06RE029%20Parental%20involvement.pdf

Ingham, R and Carrera, C (1998) 'Liaison between parents and schools on sex education policies', *Sex Education Matters,* 15, 11.

Kirby, D (2007) *Emerging Answers: Research Findings on Programs to Reduce Teen Pregnancy and Sexually Transmitted Diseases.* Washington, DC: National Campaign to Prevent Teen and Unplanned Pregnancy.

Kirkman, M, Rosenthal, DA and Feldman, SS (2005) 'Being open with your mouth shut: the meaning of "openness" in family communication about sexuality', *Sex Education,* 5, 1, 49–66.

Mumsnet (2011) Mumsnet sex education survey. http://www.mumsnet.com/campaigns/mumsnet-sex-education-survey#Results The survey was carried out between 18 and 23 November 2011 and had 1061 respondents (accessed 20 November 2012).

NFER (National Foundation for Educational Research in England and Wales) (1994) *Parents, Schools and Sex Education: A compelling case for partnership*, prepared for the Health Education Authority.

NHS Bristol (2009) 'Parent attitudes to teenage sexual health, pregnancy and sex and relationships education: Telephone interviews', MSS Research (Project number MR4689). http://www.4ypbristol.co.uk/professionals_supportparents

Ofsted (2002) *Sex and Relationships.* Northants: Ofsted.

Ofsted (2010) *Personal, Social, Health and Economic Education in Schools.* Crown Copyright, Manchester.

Ofsted (2012) The framework for school inspection from September 2012, Crown copyright http://www.ofsted.gov.uk/resources/framework-for-school-inspection-september-2012-0 (accessed 20 November 2012).

Populus (2008) Populus interviewed 580 children aged 11–14, and 535 parents of children aged 11–14, online between 9 and 12 June 2008. Populus is a member of the British Polling Council and abides by its rules. The full report is no longer available online, however selected findings are published in Naik, A (2008) *Everyday Conversations, Every Day*. London: Parents Centre/ Department for Children, Schools and Families.

Sex Education Forum (2008) *Key Findings: Young people's survey on sex and relationships education*. London: NCB.

Sex Education Forum (2010) *Does sex and relationships education work? A Sex Education Forum evidence briefing*. London: NCB.

Sherbert Research (2009) *Customer Voice Research: Sex and Relationships Education*. London: Department for Children, Schools and Families.

Turnbull. T., van Wersch, A., and van Schaik, P. (2011). A grounded theory approach to sex and relationship education in British families. *Qualitative Methods in Psychology*, 12, 41–51.

Turnbull.T., van Schaik, P and van Wersch. (2012). Communication about sexual matters within the family: Facilitators and barriers. *Health Education Journal*, 30(2), 40–47.

Walker, JL (2001) 'A qualitative study of parents' experiences of providing sex education for their children: The implications for health education', *Health Education Journal,* 60, 2, 132–46.